ESSENTIAL FITNESS

SPORTS TRAINING

BY REBECCA MORRIS

Essential Library

An Imprint of Abdo Publishing
abdobooks.com

ABDOBOOKS.COM
Published by Abdo Publishing, a division of ABDO, PO Box 398166, Minneapolis, Minnesota 55439.

Printed in the United States of America, North Mankato, Minnesota.
052024
092024

Cover Photo: Shutterstock Images
Interior Photos: Andy Devlin/National Hockey League/Getty Images, 3, 86–87; Shutterstock Images, 4–5, 16–17, 26, 30–31, 39, 51, 56–57, 59, 60, 81, 82, 89, 100–101, 101; M. Anthony Nesmith/Icon Sportswire/Getty Images, 7; Matthew J. Lee/Boston Globe/Getty Images, 8; Pete Marovich/The Washington Post/Getty Images, 11; Jill Brady/Portland Press Herald/Getty Images, 12; Jacob Kupferman/Getty Images Sport/Getty Images, 15; Cui Nan/China News Service/Getty Images, 19; David J. Griffin/Icon Sportswire/Getty Images, 21; iStockphoto, 22, 24, 33, 36, 44–45, 66, 69, 70, 90; Philip Pacheco/Anadolu Agency/Getty Images, 28–29; Alan Diaz/AP Images, 29; Nabil K. Mark/Centre Daily Times/Knight Ridder/AP Images, 35; Eddie Keogh/The FA Collection/Getty Images, 41; Matthew Stockman/Getty Images Sport/Getty Images, 42–43; William Purnell/Icon Sportswire/Getty Images, 43; Nikos Frazier/Omaha World-Herald/AP Images, 46; C. Morgan Engal/NCAA Photos/Getty Images, 50; Eric Feferberg/AFP/Getty Images, 53; Bruce Yeung/Getty Images Sport/Getty Images, 55; Darren Walsh/Chelsea FC/Getty Images, 62; Damien Meyer/AFP/Getty Images, 65; Cooper Neill/Major League Baseball/Getty Images, 72–73; Scott W. Grau/Icon Sportswire/Getty Images, 75; Marlin Levison/Star Tribune/Getty Images, 76; Mary DeCicco/Major League Baseball/Getty Images, 78; Brian Bahr/Getty Images Sport/Getty Images, 85; Dennis Pajot/Getty Images Sport/Getty Images, 93, 97; Brian Babineau/National Hockey League/Getty Images, 94; Nick Lachance/Toronto Star/Getty Images, 98

Editor: Charlie Beattie
Series Designer: Jake Slavik

Library of Congress Control Number: 2023949602

PUBLISHER'S CATALOGING-IN-PUBLICATION DATA
Names: Morris, Rebecca, author.
Title: Sports training / by Rebecca Morris
Description: Minneapolis, Minnesota: Abdo Publishing, 2025 | Series: Essential fitness | Includes online resources and index.
Identifiers: ISBN 9781098293291 (lib. bdg.) | ISBN 9798384912569 (ebook)
Subjects: LCSH: Physical education and training--Juvenile literature. | Training with weights --Juvenile literature. | Physical fitness--Juvenile literature. | Muscles--Juvenile literature. | Exercise--Juvenile literature.
Classification: DDC 613.71--dc23

CONTENTS

CHAPTER ONE
TRAINING ON THE BASKETBALL COURT 4

CHAPTER TWO
WHAT IS SPORTS TRAINING? 16

CHAPTER THREE
SPORTS TRAINING AND THE BODY 30

CHAPTER FOUR
VOLLEYBALL TRAINING 44

CHAPTER FIVE
SOCCER TRAINING 56

CHAPTER SIX
BASEBALL AND SOFTBALL TRAINING 72

CHAPTER SEVEN
ICE HOCKEY TRAINING 86

ESSENTIAL FACTS 100

GLOSSARY 102

ADDITIONAL RESOURCES 104

SOURCE NOTES 106

INDEX 110

ABOUT THE AUTHOR 112

CHAPTER

TRAINING ON THE BASKETBALL COURT

Camryn and her teammates were at practice on the court in their high school's gym. Coach Nguyen had already led them through sets of body-weight exercises, including walking lunges, squats, push-ups, planks, and burpees. The burpees were especially tough. They combined the movement of squats, planks, and jumps into one exercise.

Now the team was getting ready to work through a circuit of three drills. The first drill started at the baseline underneath one of the court's hoops. The second ran along the half-court line. The third began at the free-throw line on the

Basketball requires high levels of agility, quickness, and explosiveness.

far side of the court. Camryn bent down to retie her shoes and headed to the first drill.

RUNNING THE T-DRILL

At the first station, Camryn saw four cones arranged in the shape of a T. One cone was in the middle of the baseline. The second was 15 feet (4.6 m) straight ahead. The final two were 7.5 feet (2.3 m) to the left and right of the second cone. "Camryn, you're up first," Coach Nguyen called. They had run this drill before in practice. Camryn knew the goal was to move through the T pattern as quickly as possible.

She started at the first cone and sprinted to the cone straight ahead. From there, she bent her knees slightly and shuffled left to the third cone. This sideways movement

DYNAMIC WARM-UPS

Sports training sessions often begin with dynamic warm-ups lasting about five to ten minutes. Dynamic warm-ups prepare the body to perform sports movements safely. A dynamic warm-up for basketball may include heel walks, toe walks, and walking straight leg kicks. Dynamic warm-ups also incorporate movements similar to those players use during a game. Examples for basketball include jogging and skipping forward and backward. These movements prepare players' bodies for the running and jumping when playing basketball. Dynamic warm-ups involve motion, which makes them different from static stretching. Static stretching involves holding still in one position for as long as 45 seconds.

Basketball players need to be able to stay balanced while stopping and changing directions.

is called a lateral shuffle. Camryn faced forward, but her body moved sideways.

When Camryn reached the third cone, she changed directions and shuffled to the right. This time the lateral shuffle was twice as far. Camryn had to shuffle 15 feet (4.6 m) to the fourth cone. All the while, she maintained the slight bend in her knees.

At the fourth cone, she reversed directions again, shuffling left back to the center cone. From there, she backpedaled to return to the first cone, where she took a break. She was glad for the rest. After the initial sprint, the lateral shuffles, and the backpedaling, the muscles in her

The Euro step got its name because it was first popularized by professional players in European leagues.

hips, quadriceps, hamstrings, and calves were burning. She felt that the lateral shuffles were especially tough. They required her to maintain bent knees and engage hip muscles for 30 feet (9.1 m) of continuous movement.

The break was short, only 30 seconds. By that time, Camryn had caught her breath, and she was ready when Coach Nguyen said, "Great work. Do it again, and this time start by shuffling to the right. Switching the direction ensures that both legs get the same challenge."

BUILDING DYNAMIC POWER

Next, Camryn moved to the middle of the court for the second drill. "Are we doing shuttle runs?" her teammate Jamie asked. Camryn shrugged and said, "Probably some kind of hops. We usually use the half-court line for those." Sure enough, as the rest of the team made their way over, Coach Nguyen called out that the next drill would be Euro hop steps.

The name for this drill comes from a basketball maneuver called a Euro step. This move is when the player dodges a defender by taking a quick, sideways step in one direction and then takes another quick, sideways step in the opposite direction. The goal of the Euro hop steps drill is to alternate single-leg hops across the half-court line.

A few teammates worked through the drill before Camryn. She could tell just by watching them that this drill would be another challenge for her legs. She would have to generate enough power from just one leg to propel herself both upward and diagonally forward. She would also have to control her landings.

When her turn arrived, she stood just to the left of the half-court line and shifted all her weight to her left foot. She bent her right knee to hold her right foot in the air behind her. Then she dipped her left knee and sprang up to hop diagonally across the half-court line. She landed on her right foot. Without stopping to rest, she repeated the movement, now springing from her right foot and landing on her left. She traveled the entire length of the 50-foot (15.2 m) line.

At the end of the line, Coach Nguyen told Camryn to rest again for 30 seconds. She took a few easy steps and shook out her legs to loosen the muscles. She rotated her ankles with a few gentle turns. A timer dinged when the 30 seconds were up, and Coach Nguyen called, "Ready for the next set?" When Camryn nodded that she was, the coach tossed her a basketball. There would be a new challenge for the second set. With each hop over the line, Camryn would also move the basketball from one side of her body to the other.

Holding the basketball with both hands at waist level, Camryn positioned herself again at one end of the half-court line. "Start on the right foot this time," Coach Nguyen told her. "Remember that like with the T-drill, we want to train both sides equally."

HAND STRENGTH

Basketball players depend on their hands to dribble, pass, catch, shoot, and rebound. The human hand contains 27 bones, 27 joints, 34 muscles, and more than 100 ligaments and tendons. Just as athletes can train other parts of their bodies, they can also train their hands for strength. Examples include squeezing a tennis ball, performing push-ups from the fingertips rather than the palms, and throwing and catching a medicine ball.

Basketball players run roughly 2.5 miles (4 km) per game.

With the first hop from right foot to left, Camryn moved the ball from her right hip to her left hip. The new combination of movement required additional work to maintain balance. Camryn wobbled, so she tightened the muscles in her core to stabilize each landing. Her legs again grew tired as she approached the end of the set. Her arms did not have to generate as much power as her legs, but they were getting tired too. This set was a total body effort.

ENHANCING REACTION SPEED

Finally, Camryn went to the free-throw line at the far end of the court. Another teammate, Alia, was already there.

Rebounding in basketball combines physical ability with the anticipation of where the ball might fall after it hits the rim.

They would be partners for the third drill. Camryn stood with her back to the hoop, facing Alia. Meanwhile, Alia held a basketball and prepared to throw it over Camryn's head and against the hoop's backboard.

"With your back to the hoop, you won't see where the ball will hit," Coach Nguyen said. "We are reacting to uncertainty in this drill. Camryn, once Alia throws the ball, you turn, locate the rebound, grab it, and shoot. Take a defensive stance to get ready."

Camryn's legs were a little wider than hip-distance apart. Her knees were bent, and she was on the balls of her feet. She leaned forward slightly, ready to move. Her hands and arms were spread wide at her sides. She began shuffling left and right in defensive slides.

Alia dribbled a few times and then threw the ball toward the backboard. As soon as the ball was thrown, Camryn turned. She saw the ball strike the right side of the backboard. Camryn darted to the spot and extended her

MENTAL TOUGHNESS

Experts recommend mental as well as physical training in sports. Mental training helps athletes set goals and develop the mindset that achieving goals takes hard work. It also helps them build the resilience to face losses in games and handle tough workouts. Lessons stressing mental toughness might include shifting focus from winning to the fun of playing and seeing mistakes as opportunities to learn. This can turn setbacks into what former UCLA men's basketball coach John Wooden called "stepping stones to achievement."[1]

right arm to reach for the ball. It skimmed her fingertips, a little too high to catch.

The ball hit the floor, but Camryn scrambled after it, grabbing it just before it went out of bounds. She dribbled a few times, took aim, and released a jump shot. The ball banked off the backboard and dropped through the net.

GAME TIME

In the first game of the season, Camryn and her team were down one point against a strong defensive team. Playing power forward, Camryn caught a pass and looked for an opening. There was none. She bounded left, then right, trying to escape the defensive pressure, and shot the ball. It was a miss. Jamie grabbed the rebound on the opposite side of the net and powered into a jump shot. Jamie's shot was also a miss.

Camryn reacted and pivoted to get in front of the defender. She grabbed the rebound, but with no open shot, she sent the ball to a guard. Camryn backpedaled to get some space. No other players were open, so the guard passed the ball back. The defender advanced again, so Camryn turned her back to the hoop.

She shuffled right, then quickly left. The footwork was fast enough to cut around the defender. Camryn drove into the opening and floated the ball toward the basket. It sank through the hoop for two points, giving her team

Top athletes put in hours of practice in order to be their best during competitive games.

the lead. The drills she ran during practice prepared her to make this key play. Camryn took a mental note to thank Coach Nguyen later for helping sharpen her quickness, power, and reaction speed.

WHAT IS SPORTS TRAINING?

Sports training develops the skills athletes need for a particular sport. Training programs vary based on the requirements of each sport. They also depend on the athlete's experience, skill level, goals, and age.

Student athletes, recreational athletes, and professional athletes all participate in sports training. Athletes today have support from a range of experts. These experts include coaches, physical therapists, strength and conditioning professionals, athletic trainers, nutritionists, biomechanical engineers, neurologists, sports scientists, and orthopedic doctors.

Athletes training for specific sports focus on strength and stamina.

ATHLETE AGE

For sports training, there are multiple ways to think about an athlete's age. Sport-specific training age is the length of time an athlete has worked in their sport. Chronological age is the number of years since birth. Developmental age refers to the maturity of a person's body. For example, people reach their full height within a range of ages during adolescence, but the exact age will vary from person to person. Well-designed sports training programs look at athletes as individuals and consider all these measurements of age.

THE HISTORY OF SPORTS TRAINING

People from many ancient cultures incorporated sports into their lives and practiced to improve performance. Ancient Egyptians weight trained with heavy sandbags. They practiced long-distance running and field sports such as high jumps. To challenge their jumping ability, athletes sat on the ground across from each other and held their hands and feet at shoulder height as obstacles for others to hurdle.

Many cultures also practiced early forms of sports still played today, including handball, boxing, and rhythmic gymnastics. In ancient China, military training exercises for strength and stamina developed into training for recreational sports. One of them was a soccer-like game called cuju.

In ancient Greece, the Olympics occurred regularly from 776 BCE to 393 CE, with some competitions continuing into the 400s CE. Olympic training developed

Young players in traditional costumes play the sport of cuju. The object of the game is to keep the ball in the air as long as possible.

from the practice of daily activities, such as the agricultural work of digging and pulling carts, into organized systems of endurance and strength training. Endurance training included swimming and running. Speed training involved racing against animals.

Strength training included bending iron bars, lifting stone blocks, balancing weighted balls, and pushing bags filled with flour, seeds, or sand. Athletes climbed ropes and carried partners on sloping terrain. They varied intervals and practiced agile footwork. Trainers developed a four-day system called tetrads. Each day focused on a different kind of training and intensity. Every third day was a rest day.

Interest in sports training has continued into modern times. In the United States, the first professional athletic trainer was James Robinson, hired by Harvard University in 1881. In 1950, the National Athletic Trainers' Association (NATA) was created. Several other national and international professional societies were also established throughout the 1900s.

The kinds of strength and plyometric training common in sports training today are relatively new. These techniques gained popularity in the late 1970s and 1980s. Fields dedicated to studying sports nutrition, recovery, and sports psychology also emerged around that time.

PREHAB

In sports training, prehabilitation, or prehab for short, is an injury prevention strategy. The term comes from the word rehabilitation, which is treatment to restore function and athletic skill after an injury. Prehab often uses many of the same exercises as rehabilitation, but athletes in prehab practice these exercises before injury occurs as a way to reduce risk. Prehab exercises focus on mobility, flexibility, balance, coordination, and stability. Prehab not only reduces injury risk but also builds a foundation for agility.

FORMS OF SPORTS TRAINING TODAY

Sports training today uses periodization to help athletes progress from a base level of general fitness to optimal performance. Periodization breaks training into cycles of weeks or months. These cycles typically build toward a sports season or competitive event. They are also broken up into heavier and lighter periods. The lighter sessions are known as "deloading." According to fitness expert Sharon Gam, periodization "includes strategic recovery periods to make sure your body adapts properly."[1] The objective of periodization is to reduce injury risk by allowing the body enough time to adapt and recover from increasingly difficult training.

The first phase develops a foundation of strength and aerobic fitness. Experts advise base strength training

The National Football League's preseason practice schedule is an example of periodization, as players slowly work to get in peak shape before the season begins.

Weight training exercises can be tailored to focus on strength or endurance.

for all athletes, even those in endurance sports such as marathon running. Base strength training protects joints, muscles, ligaments, and tendons. It gives athletes the foundation for more intense speed and power training in later phases. Similarly, experts recommend all athletes develop an aerobic base of endurance, even those whose positions focus on short bursts of power, such as football linemen. Base aerobic training improves the body's ability to recover from the challenges of strength, speed, and power training.

Base strength training targets major muscle groups with isolation and compound exercises. Isolation exercises work one muscle group at a time. Bicep curls are an example of this. Compound exercises work multiple joints and muscle groups. Squats, for example, work several groups of muscles in the legs.

Base strength training also focuses on balancing opposing muscles, such as the quadriceps and hamstrings in the front and back of each leg, respectively. Common exercises for base strength training in many sports include lunges, squats, step-ups, calf raises, push-ups, rows, leg presses, chest presses, and planks. Training in this phase uses light weights and works toward higher repetitions.

Aerobic exercise involves continuous activity at a consistent pace. Cycling, swimming, and running are examples. Aerobic base training is also called steady-state training because the body maintains the activity for an extended time, typically 20 minutes or more. Athletes ride stationary bikes, walk or jog on treadmills, or swim to build aerobic base.

After the base training phase, athletes progress to heavier weights for strength training and increase their volume of aerobic training as needed. This phase applies the concept of specificity, which means that the training focuses on the skills demanded by the athlete's sport and position. The gradual increases in training are called progressive overload.

The next training phase is called strength/power. Movements are fast and explosive. This training phase uses plyometric exercises and high-intensity intervals to build power. Common plyometric exercises used to train for many sports include box jumps, single- and double-leg hopping, leaping with long strides from one leg to the other, and throwing weighted balls against the ground or walls. Sprint intervals are a common method to build speed.

The strength/power phase also focuses on agility and quickness. Speedy, agile athletes can change direction at high speed with balance and control, allowing them to react quickly in fast-paced situations. This kind of training is essential to both improving performance and reducing injury risk. Many sports use cone and ladder training to build agility and quickness through varied drills that involve footwork, hopping, jumping, and sprinting.

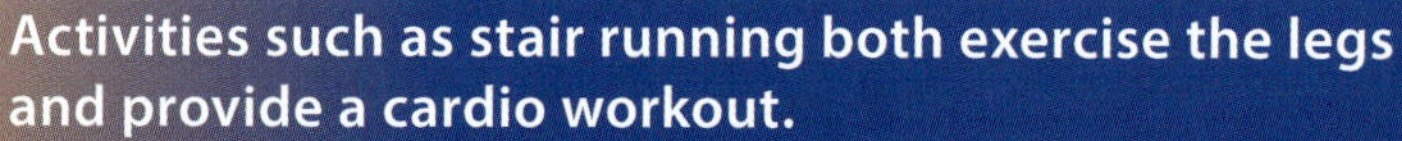

Activities such as stair running both exercise the legs and provide a cardio workout.

The in-season segment is also known as the competition phase. These workouts maintain the strength and power built in earlier phases. However, training volume is decreased to reduce fatigue and maximize competitive performance.

When the season ends, athletes take a break from their sport for several weeks. Experts recommend cross-training during the offseason phase of the periodization cycle. For example, a soccer team might play recreational water polo, or a football player might cross-train with yoga, Pilates, or dance. Well-designed sports programs today also integrate guidance for mental health, nutrition, and rest to complement physical training in all phases.

PROFESSIONAL ATHLETE TRAINING

Many athletes preparing for competition incorporate two training sessions per day. The first will often take place in the morning and the second in the afternoon. One session involves practicing the sport. A skier would spend time on a mountain, a swimmer would be in a pool, and a rugby player would be on a field. Often, the second session will focus on overall strength, cardio, or flexibility and mobility. Athletes eat between training sessions, and many take a nap. They may also review performance videos with coaches. After training, athletes use healthy recovery techniques.

TRAINING FACILITIES AND GEAR

Sports training locations include gyms and sport-specific fields, tracks, rinks, and pools. Some sport training

Cones and agility ladders take up very little room, which makes them easy to use anywhere.

activities require no equipment. Athletes do not need equipment for body-weight exercises such as push-ups or plyometric exercises such as jumping and sprinting.

Other activities require minimal equipment, such as free weights, kettlebells, medicine balls, balance boards and pads, elastic bands, steps, and boxes. Cones, agility ladders, jump ropes, and hurdles are common, low-cost, and easy-to-transport equipment for agility and quickness drills. For timed drills, athletes use handheld digital timers, watches, or other devices.

Athletes also train with gym equipment as well as sport-specific weight equipment. Gym equipment commonly used in sports training includes cables, squat racks or cages, weight machines, and sleds. Examples of sport-specific equipment include blocking sleds for football linemen and weighted bats for baseball and softball hitters.

Training incorporates drills with equipment specific to the sport, such as tennis rackets, lacrosse sticks, or golf clubs. Athletes may also complete some of their training using sport-specific protective equipment. Items such as helmets, cleats, pads, guards, gloves, mouthguards, or goggles would all fit into this category.

Training can also include wearable technology that tracks biomechanics and biometrics. Biomechanics is how the body performs athletic movements, such as landing technique in running or stroke technique in swimming. Biometrics are measures of how systems in the body are working. For example, heart rate is a piece of biometric data that helps gauge an athlete's energy use and fatigue.

Wristbands and smartwatches are some of the most common wearable devices, and companies have begun developing smart clothing and shoes. Elite athletes may also wear vests or leg straps that hold sensors. Coaches may record training sessions using cameras and other sensors to analyze athletes' biomechanics.

SPORTS TRAINING IN VIRTUAL REALITY

In 2015, a few college football programs began using virtual reality (VR) sports to complement their training. Since then, VR has become part of training in many other college programs and professional sports leagues. There are also platforms for younger athletes and recreational athletes.

In VR sports training, athletes wear headsets to immerse themselves in a virtual environment. They may also attach sensors to their equipment. These sensors track real-life movement and show it in the virtual space.

For example, a baseball VR system has an optional sensor that can be attached to a bat. Batters can then practice their swing against hundreds of virtual pitches and get analysis on their mechanics from live coaches. "It's visualization times a million," said former Stanford University football kicker Conrad Ukropina.[2]

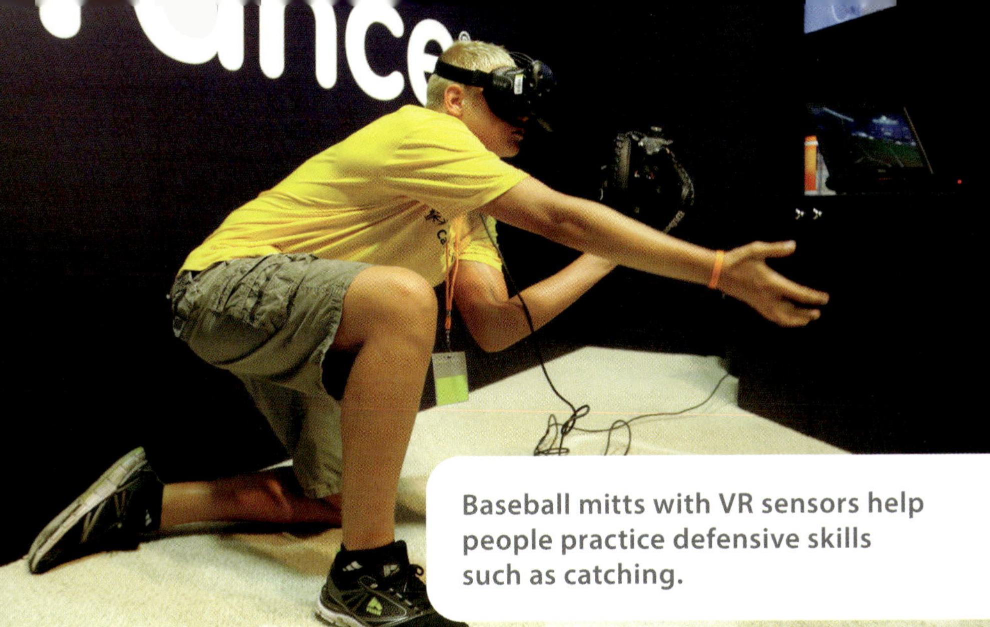

Baseball mitts with VR sensors help people practice defensive skills such as catching.

Elite teams may also have haptic technology as part of their VR systems. Haptic technology generates vibrations or forces meant to simulate the sensation of touch or contact with equipment. A soccer player training in VR with a haptic system would be able to feel that they were kicking a real ball.

Experts believe VR training will continue to evolve and become more realistic and widely available. One key benefit is increased practice with decreased risk of injury. VR lets athletes practice technique without impact. Experts say this can be especially useful for contact sports such as basketball and football.

VR also lets athletes practice when training facilities or partners are not available. In addition, VR can provide reaction drills and cognitive drills to train for mental parts of competition, such as decision making. Alongside these known benefits, experts also emphasize the need for ongoing and long-term research to study the effects of VR on sports training.

CHAPTER

SPORTS TRAINING AND THE BODY

Sports training changes and develops the parts of the body needed for peak sports performance. Changes created during training are called adaptations. The effects of sports training depend on the type of training that is being performed.

Programs combine aerobic training, anaerobic training, and recovery techniques to meet an athlete's individual and sport-specific needs. Well-designed sports training programs have a number of benefits. Some are designed to give athletes an edge in competition. Others can reduce the risk of injury.

Training for any sporting event involves a great deal of repetition.

AEROBIC TRAINING

Aerobic means "with oxygen." During aerobic training, oxygen initiates chemical reactions that convert nutrients stored in the body's cells into energy. Aerobic training first burns glucose, a form of sugar. Glucose is stored as glycogen in muscles. The liver also stores glycogen, which releases into the bloodstream as blood glucose. Muscles will use some of this blood glucose as well as their own glycogen stores during exercise.

In aerobic training, the body begins to burn fat after 30 to 60 minutes. Fat contains more energy potential than glucose, but it converts into energy more slowly and requires more oxygen for conversion. The body stores fat in the muscles and other parts of the body, and these stores break down into fatty acids for energy during exercise. Blood flow supplies the muscles with fatty acids from other parts of the body, glucose from the liver, and oxygen from the lungs.

One benefit of regular aerobic training is that the body becomes more efficient at using fat as energy. This adaptation increases endurance, and it helps preserve the body's glycogen stores. Another effect of aerobic training is that it improves the cardiovascular system. Aerobic exercise makes the heart stronger and more efficient. Blood vessels also become larger, and the body grows new capillaries in the skeletal muscles.

These changes improve blood flow, making the body better at delivering oxygen and nutrients to muscles. The body also uses this oxygen more efficiently. With these adaptations, muscles can endure longer periods of exercise and recover more quickly afterward.

Muscles are composed of different types of fibers. They are called slow-twitch, or type I, and fast-twitch, or type II, fibers. The "twitch" refers to how quickly or how often a muscle contracts when in use. Slow-twitch fibers are capable of the prolonged contraction needed for continuous aerobic activity. They also support the sustained muscle contractions necessary for good posture and stability.

Running is a popular form of aerobic training.

Fast-twitch muscle fibers are larger than slow-twitch fibers. They can also generate more strength and power, though they cannot contract for as long as slow-twitch fibers. Aerobic training strengthens slow-twitch fibers, and it also supports recovery and endurance in fast-twitch fibers.

ANAEROBIC TRAINING

Anaerobic means "without oxygen." Sometimes an activity uses energy at a pace faster than the body can metabolize oxygen. During this kind of activity, muscles burn their stored glucose without oxygen in a process called anaerobic glycolysis. This process provides quick bursts of energy for high-intensity movements such as sprints, jumps, and heavy weight lifting.

Anaerobic training occurs closer to an athlete's maximum heart rate than aerobic training. Aerobic training occurs

BONE STRENGTH

Like other parts of the body, bones adapt to training. Weight lifting and plyometric training, such as jumping, are anaerobic activities that build bone strength. Weight-bearing aerobic exercise also strengthens bone. These aerobic activities work against gravity and are performed from standing positions. Walking and running are examples. The Orthopedic & Sports Medicine Institute in Texas explains, "During weight-bearing activity, the muscles and tendons apply tension to the bones, which stimulates the bones to produce more bone tissue."[1] The added tissue makes bones stronger.

Physical sports such as football require regular weight-lifting training to both build and maintain strength.

at 60 to 80 percent of maximum heart rate. Anaerobic training happens at 80 to 90 percent of maximum heart rate.[2]

The body can perform anaerobic glycolysis for only short periods of time. The high-intensity movements of anaerobic exercise last between just a few seconds and a maximum of three minutes. Athletes recognize they have reached their limit when they feel out of breath and their muscles burn. They must take breaks before repeating anaerobic exercise. Regular anaerobic sports training

Healthy eating is a vital part of post-exercise recovery.

allows the body to adapt and support longer periods of high-intensity effort.

Another adaptation to anaerobic training is an increase in the size of fast-twitch muscle fibers. This adaptation is called hypertrophy. Hypertrophy occurs when the stress of anaerobic training creates microtears in muscle fibers. During recovery, the body heals these microtears by regenerating tissue and fusing new, larger muscle fibers. Orthopedic surgeon Michael Karns explains, "You have to break muscle down to build it back up stronger."[3]

THE IMPORTANCE OF RECOVERY

The body can adapt both positively and negatively to sports training. Positive adaptations increase tolerance for exercise, improve sport performance, and reduce injury risk. The negative changes are called maladaptations. Maladaptations can lead to exhaustion, decreased performance, and a higher chance of injury. Recovery techniques encourage positive adaptations and reduce risk of maladaptations. Recovery includes proper nutrition, adequate hydration, enough sleep, and regular stretching.

Athletes need to consume enough nutrients to meet their energy needs and training demands. There are macronutrients and micronutrients. The three macronutrients are carbohydrates, fats, and proteins. Carbohydrates and fats are important for energy. Protein is essential for muscle growth and repair. Foods such as whole grains and fruit provide carbohydrates, nut butters and oils contain fats, and dairy, fish, meat, and beans are rich in protein.

Some foods are sources of more than one macronutrient. Nut butters, for example, provide both protein and fat. Micronutrients are vitamins and minerals such as calcium, vitamin D, and iron that the body needs in smaller quantities than macronutrients.

MIXING INTENSITIES

There can be crossover in aerobic and anaerobic training during workouts. Intentionally mixing the two systems in one workout is a strategy used to increase tolerance for high-intensity sports performance. Mixing jogging and sprinting intervals is one example. Jogging at a steady, low-intensity pace provides aerobic training. Short, high-speed sprints provide anaerobic training.

NEUROMUSCULAR TRAINING

The neuromuscular system consists of muscles and nerves. Movement occurs when nerve cells send signals from the brain to muscles. Over time, muscles develop patterns and habits, which are known as muscle memory. Neuromuscular training focuses on creating movement patterns with optimal biomechanics. Athletes who jump frequently in sports such as basketball and volleyball train their landings to ensure knees align with their feet rather than collapsing inward. Optimizing biomechanics improves performance and decreases the risk of injury to vulnerable tissues such as ligaments and cartilage.

The quantities needed of both types of nutrients depend on the athlete and the sport. As guidelines for general health, the National Institutes of Health advise that 45 to 65 percent of daily calories come from carbohydrates, 25 to 35 percent come from fat, and 10 to 35 percent come from protein.[4] For all athletes, experts recommend planning out balanced meals and snacks that include a wide range of foods. Athletes should also plan out when to eat so they have enough energy for training and fuel for recovery. If athletes have trouble meeting nutrition requirements, sports nutritionists and registered dieticians can advise on meal planning and supplements.

Drinking plenty of water to stay hydrated is a crucial part of training and staying healthy. Hydration maintains organ function, brain function, and body temperature.

Training causes athletes to lose water through sweating and breathing. They must hydrate to avoid negative impacts on health and performance such as decreased blood flow, dizziness, confusion, and overheating.

Like nutrition, each person's exact hydration needs vary. The temperature conditions also impact hydration requirements. Training in hot weather causes more sweating and requires more hydration than training in cool weather.

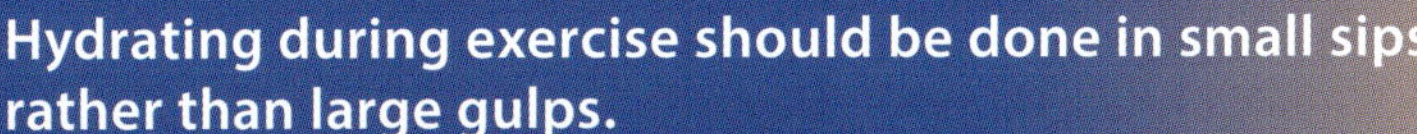

Hydrating during exercise should be done in small sips rather than large gulps.

As a baseline, experts advise that athletes drink water regularly throughout the day, follow the recommended daily intake for their age group, and then be mindful of hydration during training. For ages 14 to 18, NATA's daily recommendation is ten cups (2.4 L) of water for females and fourteen cups (3.3 L) for males. For ages 9 to 13, the recommendation is nine cups (2.1 L) for females and ten cups (2.4 L) for males. A guideline for additional sport hydration is one cup (0.2 L) every 15 to 20 minutes.[5]

Registered dieticians and nutritionists can advise athletes on how to hydrate before, during, and after training without drinking too little or too much water. Consuming too much water can cause dangerously low levels of sodium in the body. These experts can also offer guidance on when hydration through water alone is sufficient and when other kinds of drinks may be useful.

Sleep is another important recovery aspect. During sleep, the body repairs tissue stressed by sports training. Hormones promote this recovery, and insufficient sleep can cause imbalances in hormones such as human growth hormone and testosterone. These hormones are released during sleep. With lack of sleep, their amounts can decrease, and they may slow tissue regeneration.

In addition, lack of sleep affects the body's ability to use nutrients for energy during training and repair tissue after training. Cognitive effects from lack of sleep

Pre- and post-training stretching is often tailored to the muscles used in a specific sport.

include decreased reaction time and decision-making ability, which are crucial skills in sports performance. Experts recommend nine to ten hours of sleep per night for athletes.

Stretching increases blood flow throughout the body to speed physical and mental recovery. Experts suggest athletes incorporate stretching before and after training. In an article for the National Academy of Sports Medicine's website, neuroscientist Allison Brager explains, "Full-body mobility and stretching such as many of the positions and movement flows adopted and practiced during yoga can also [improve] mood and enhance cognitive performance."[6]

ENHANCING PERFORMANCE WITH GEAR

Athletic companies often claim their gear improves performance beyond what is possible with the human body alone. Sometimes these claims are marketing strategies, but sometimes they can show real-world results. This kind of innovation happened with football gloves in the 1990s. A Canadian football player researched materials for better receiving gloves, which led to the silicone surfaces used in gloves today. One study found the silicone surface to be "about 20 percent stickier than a human hand."[7] Players at all levels use them to improve their catching ability. They especially help with one-handed catches.

The gloves are legal in National Football League (NFL) play, but some gear is banned from competition because it could offer an unfair advantage. In 2010, the National Basketball Association (NBA) banned shoes designed with soles to enhance jumping ability. The company behind the shoes, Athletic Propulsion Labs, called the design Load 'N Launch technology. Elite running competitions have also banned certain kinds of performance-enhancing shoes, and the Olympics have banned some swimsuit designs.

Many hours of scientific study and innovation go into sports equipment such as gloves and football helmets.

Some question the place of this kind of gear in competitive sports. Marathoner Tegla Loroupe, a Kenyan runner who once held a world record, criticized shoes with performance-improving technology as "cheating . . . because you don't use your own strength."[8] Others argue the gear helps athletes push the limits of sport performance and opens new possibilities.

Companies continue researching new technology. In 2021, Rawlings released a baseball glove created using 3D printing. Rawlings and its partner companies claim the flexible, lighter design gives players more control and quicker reaction ability compared with traditional gloves.

Consumer companies are not the only ones that innovate performance gear. Professors and students in university engineering labs also create performance gear alongside protective gear, prosthetics for Para athletes, and other sports equipment.

CHAPTER

VOLLEYBALL TRAINING

Volleyball is the most popular team sport for US girls and women in high school and college. There are also male teams and mixed-gender teams. Indoor volleyball is the most common version, but there are variations such as beach volleyball, sitting volleyball, deaf volleyball, and more.

Volleyball began as a low-impact alternative to basketball when physical educator William G. Morgan of Massachusetts invented the sport in 1895. Since then, volleyball has developed into a high-impact sport that requires explosive power from its players. The primary skills needed to play volleyball include service, serve reception, setting, attacking, blocking, passing, and digging.

More than 450,000 girls participated in high school volleyball during the 2021–22 school year. About 66,000 boys also competed.

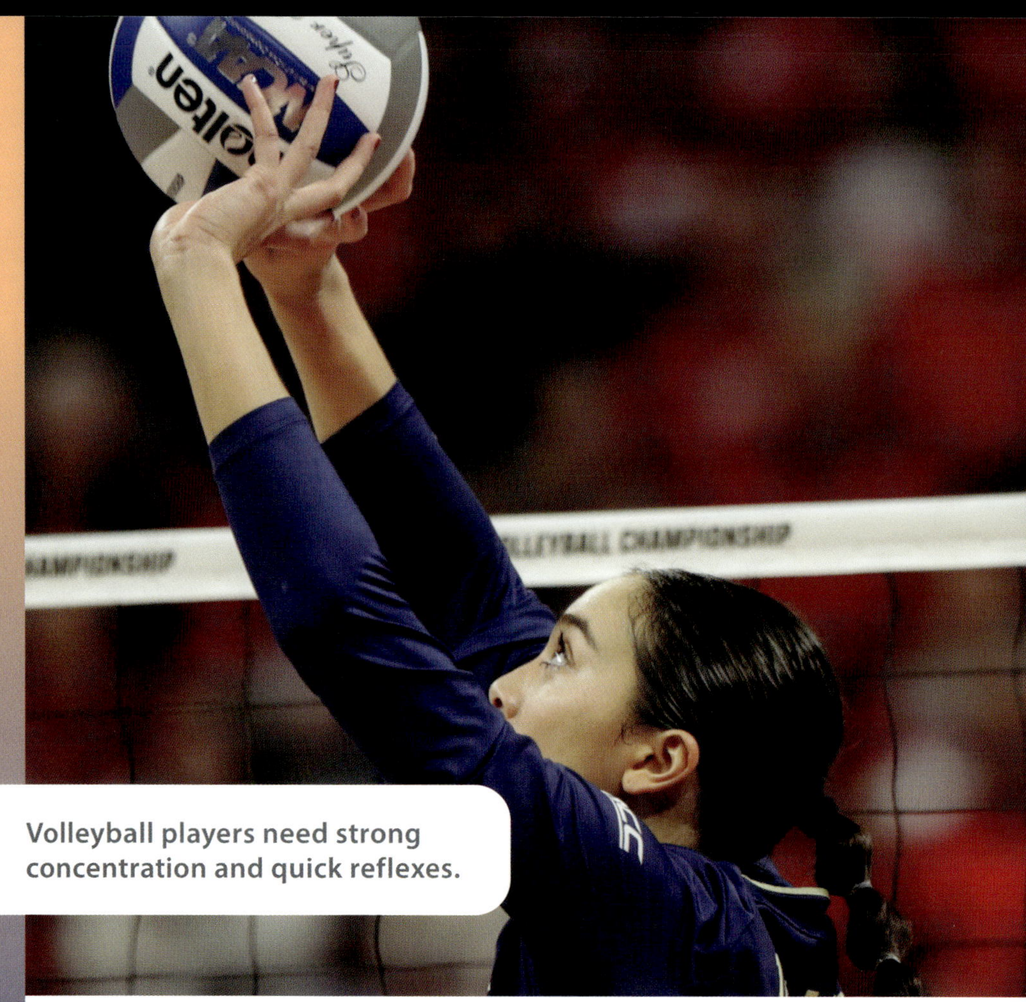

Volleyball players need strong concentration and quick reflexes.

FIRST-STEP QUICKNESS

The book *Volleyball Skills & Drills* by the American Volleyball Coaches Association points out that the smallest playing area of team sports is the volleyball half court. Each side of a court covers about 900 square feet (84 sq m). By comparison, half of a professional basketball court covers about 2,300 square feet (214 sq m).[1] Volleyball is also unique in its fast-paced series of ball contacts, each lasting less than a second.

The small playing area and fast rallies mean players must execute plays quickly with controlled power. Coaches and trainers emphasize first-step quickness to meet the sport's unique demands. First steps are the player's initial move in reaction to a spike, tip, block, pass, or other gameplay scenario. Training incorporates a variety of drills for fast and agile footwork.

BRAIN TRAINING FOR REACTION SPEED

Visualization is a mental exercise that can improve on-court reaction speed. Athletes rehearse their gameplay by imagining various scenarios and how they would respond. Players may imagine the sound of sneakers squeaking against the floor, the feel of air around the body in a jump or dive, or the weight of the ball on their fingertips. They can envision themselves taking fast action to read opponents, defend, and attack. Envisioning success in these scenarios is important to the exercise. Performance coach Eli Straw says, "A scene is created in your mind, directed by you to play out in the manner you decide."[2]

One simple drill is the quick feet drill. Begin in an athletic stance. Your feet should be shoulder-width apart, your knees bent slightly, your back straight, your upper body leaning slightly forward, and your arms bent as if you were running. Run in place, focusing on light, quick foot strikes and staying light on your toes. Work on building up the drill's intensity and duration.

The clock drill adds a multidirectional component. Picture yourself at the center of a clock. Then move your feet to various positions on the clock. Twelve o'clock means stepping one foot forward. Six o'clock means one foot steps back. Three o'clock is right and nine o'clock is left. Other numbers are diagonal steps. For example, four o'clock is right and angled back. Follow sequences or call out numbers with a partner.

Other drills combine footwork with additional volleyball-specific actions. One easy example is partner passing. One player tosses a ball underhand, and the other player passes it back. The first player can toss the ball short or deep and also to alternate sides. Because of these variations, the passer must react and move forward, backward, laterally, and diagonally.

There are many other variations of partner passing. One partner can do an overhead throw rather than an underhand toss. The overhead throw challenges reaction time more than the underhand toss. In other

READING ANGLES IN DEFENSE

Volleyball players train to watch opponents' body language so they can position themselves to make a defensive play. Watching the approach angle and the direction of the hitter's feet, hips, and shoulders is crucial. When the hitter approaches the net straight on with hips and shoulders squared forward, defenders prepare for the spiked ball to come down the line. When the hitter's approach and body are angled, the ball will follow the angle. For example, if the hitter is angled to their right, the ball will travel to the left side of the opposing team's court.

variations, the passer begins with their eyes closed or their back turned until the partner gives an audible cue, such as "Go!"

For an additional agility challenge, partners stand on opposite sides of the court, each about two steps away from the net. One partner tosses the ball low under the net, about knee height, to the other player. This variation requires players to practice quick footwork and solid passing skills even when there is a change to their center of mass.

Center of mass is where the body's weight is concentrated. In this passing drill variation, your center of mass drops low and shifts left, right, or forward depending on where the toss travels. A more difficult version of this drill requires partners to exchange passes under the net for as long as they can.

TRAINING TO JUMP, DIG, AND PASS

Volleyball players need to jump high for spikes and blocks, but they must also be able to drop low to dig and pass. Leg strength provides a foundation for these skills. Volleyball uses a variety of leg-strengthening exercises. Some of the most common are squats and lunges because they train multiple joints and muscles in the lower body at once. They also engage and strengthen the core. Core strength provides balance and control in jumping,

Players in the libero position often have to dig the ball to keep points alive.

digging, and passing, and it generates explosive power for jumps.

Squats work the muscles in and around the legs, including the glutes, quadriceps, calves, and hamstrings, along with the obliques in your core. They also train hip mobility and knee flexibility to protect your joints during dynamic movement. When lunging, one leg steps forward, backward, or laterally. This movement trains your lower body muscles while adding a challenge to balance. Power develops from the effort to push your leg back to the starting position. There are many variations for both squats and lunges. Start with basic versions before progressing to more advanced variations.

A lateral lunge with a press is a variation that involves volleyball-specific demands of leg strength, lateral

FITNESS SNAPSHOT

SQUAT

movement, and total body stability. Begin in standing position and hold a dumbbell, weighted plate, or medicine ball close to your chest. Keeping your right foot in place, step your left leg to the side, bending that knee and shifting your hips down and back as in a squat. Most of your body weight will be in your left heel, and your right leg will remain straight. Also, your toes should face forward, and your bent left knee should align with your toes as you lower.

Keep your core braced and your back straight so your hips and shoulders stay level. While in the lunge, slowly push the weight forward until your arms are extended and parallel with the floor. Then, slowly pull the weight back toward your chest. Push off your bent leg to return to starting position. Repeat sets on one side at a time or alternate sides. Build to three sets of ten on each leg.

Jumping drills help build explosive power. Double-leg hops also incorporate agility training when players move diagonally left and right over a line of cones. Begin with three cones for young or new volleyball players and progress to five cones or more for older or more experienced players.

With this drill, players practice controlled landings during dynamic shifts in body weight. Players should bend at both the hips and knees when landing. This helps cushion the impact and protect joints. Volleyball camp

Top female volleyball players can spike the ball between 50–70 miles per hour (80–113 kmh).

director Brenna Berkimer says, "One of the most valuable things I was told by my high school weights coach was to land softly."[3]

TRAINING TO SPIKE AND SERVE

Coaches often compare the motions of spiking and serving to pulling a bow and arrow or cracking a whip. The movement involves torque, a twisting motion that produces power. When serving or spiking, a player's body rotates through the hips and torso. College coach Marie Zidek explains that serving or spiking is "transferring power from the core to the upper body."[4] Training focuses on developing this rotation and energy transfer while also strengthening the upper body and core muscles.

MEDICINE BALL THROWS FOR SETTERS

Medicine ball throws can be used to train the overhead motion of setting. In this variation, toss the ball high into the air against a wall. Begin with your feet shoulder-width apart and hold a soft medicine ball in both hands. Your elbows should be at about chest height, and the ball should be in front of your face. Bend through your knees and hips. Maintain good posture by keeping your back straight and drawing in your core. Raise to standing and throw the ball high. Your motion should be fluid though your legs and arms.

Ball slams are a simple but challenging exercise to train that energy transfer. Begin standing with your feet about shoulder-width apart. Hold a soft medicine ball or slam ball at chest height with both hands.

Keeping your back straight, engage your core and raise the ball overhead until your arms are fully extended. In one fast, explosive motion, pull your arms down to slam the ball to the ground. Your knees should bend so that your upper body hinges forward from the hips during the downward motion. Work toward three sets of ten.

Woodchoppers with a medicine ball or dumbbell train both energy transfer and rotation. Begin in a squat position with your feet shoulder-width apart. Hold the weight in both hands to the outside of one knee. Keep your arms and back straight. Push through your legs to raise from the squat while also moving the weight upward and across your body. Stop when the weight extends

Players often use a jump serve when they are looking for more power.

directly above your opposite shoulder. Reverse the motion to return to the starting position. Work toward three sets of eight on each side. In rotation exercises such as woodchoppers, proper form is important to protect your back and knees. Rotation comes through your torso, not from twisting your knees. Be sure to engage your core so you don't rotate too quickly or too far.

SOCCER TRAINING

Soccer is the world's most popular sport. There are more than 240 million players around the world and billions of fans.[1] Modern soccer has precursors in games played throughout history, including a Native American game called Pasuckquakkohowog. European colonists observed the game in 1620. Today, soccer's essential skills include collecting (receiving), dribbling, passing, shooting, defending, and heading. Running is also essential. Additionally, goalkeepers need to develop quick reflexes and strong hands.

TRAINING FOR SOCCER ENDURANCE

Soccer games are 60 to 90 minutes. In that time, a typical youth player may run several miles. A professional player may run more than

Soccer players must stay in top shape and master several technical skills.

NECK STRENGTH FOR HEADING

US Soccer, the governing body for the sport in the United States, prohibits heading for players ages ten or younger. Youth players over that age are allowed to head, but heading practice and the total number of headers allowed per week are limited. Still, heading is discouraged until after puberty or until at least 14 years of age, whichever is older. These rules seek to reduce risk of head injury. Similar to debates in other sports, the soccer world has debated how to prioritize player safety within sport-specific skills. For athletes who practice heading, research emphasizes learning proper technique from a qualified coach as well as strengthening neck muscles. Shoulder shrugs while holding a dumbbell in each hand are an example of a neck-strengthening exercise.

eight miles (12.9 km).[2] The running is not continuous. There are many starts, stops, and quick bursts. This kind of running is called varied running or broken-pace running. To meet soccer's physical demands, players train for a base of aerobic fitness as well as explosive quickness for sprints.

To develop an aerobic base, experts recommend athletes build toward steady-state runs of 40 to 60 minutes.[3] A steady-state pace is one that athletes can maintain without feeling out of breath. Athletes can begin with shorter runs to build up stamina. Steady-state runs are recommended once or twice a week. This kind of training prepares the body to be active throughout the length of a game.

Sprint drills and plyometrics train for bursts of speed. These bursts last only seconds, but players must be able to execute them many times throughout games. Sprint repeats are a simple drill. In this drill, players repeat five to ten high-speed sprints with rest between each set of sprints. A recommended sprint distance for each interval is 30 to 75 yards (27–69 m) but can vary depending on the athlete's experience.[4]

Midfielders run nearly three miles (5 km) more per match than other players.

FITNESS SNAPSHOT

JUMP ROPE

Keep posture tall and spine neutral

Keep elbows and shoulders still

Keep knees slightly bent

Keep hands the same distance from body

Land softly on balls of the feet

Explode off the ground

Fartlek runs, which get their name from the Swedish term for "speed play," combine steady-state running and sprinting. Players alternate jogging and sprinting along sides of the soccer field. Fartlek runs prepare players for the varied running speeds necessary in games.

Plyometric exercises complement run training. One example is skipping, which re-inforces proper run mechanics. Aim to skip 30 to 50 yards (27–46 m) for two to three sets. To progress to power skipping, increase your speed and focus on exploding from the ground. Begin with two sets of ten to fifteen power skips. Work toward three or four sets for 20 to 50 yards (18–46 m). Jumping rope is another simple plyometric exercise. It trains your ankles' ligaments and tendons to handle running on soccer fields.

ACCELERATING AND DECELERATING

Acceleration, when an athlete speeds up to make a play, is exciting to watch and often receives more attention than deceleration or slowing down. But high-intensity decelerations actually occur more often than high-intensity accelerations in soccer. Deceleration gives a player more agility when changing direction and transitioning into a pass or a shot.

High-intensity deceleration also tends to put more mechanical stress on the body than acceleration.

Researchers have found that the force of an athlete's deceleration is about 37 percent greater than for acceleration.[5] Training helps the body to absorb this force safely, which is important for injury prevention.

Training can incorporate deceleration into sprint drills. Put cones at five, ten, and fifteen yards (4.6, 9.1, and 13.7 m) from the start. Sprint toward the five-yard cone and come to a stop. To stop safely, shorten your stride when nearing the cone and lower your center of mass. Your hips should be back in a squat position, feet should be parallel, and knees should be bent and in line with your feet. Return to start and repeat to the ten- and fifteen-yard cones. In a variation of this drill, you can

Levi Colwill, *left*, of Chelsea FC practices dribbling around an opponent with a teammate.

decelerate into a split stance, which is a lunge with one leg bent in front of the other.

Deceleration can also be incorporated into skill drills to prepare for gameplay scenarios. Stand five to ten yards (4.6–9.1 m) away from a partner. As you run toward your partner, have them toss you a ball. Practice controlling the ball as you decelerate. This drill can be adjusted to practice passing or shooting. It can also be used by goalkeepers as a way to practice making saves.

Building leg strength and stability is also essential for safe acceleration and deceleration. Strengthening muscles to support knee bending is a particular area of focus, especially for deceleration. Step-downs using plyometric boxes are common exercises because they build quadriceps strength, and the quadriceps control knee bending. Boxes are usually two to eight inches (5–20 cm) tall. The taller the box, the more challenging the exercise is. Squats and box drops are other helpful exercises.

To perform step-downs, stand with one leg on a box. The other is straight down at the side of the box with your toes brought up. In a controlled manner, lower your leg on the box into a shallow squat until the heel of your other leg lightly taps the floor. Rise back up to the starting position through your stance leg. Your hips and shoulders should be level throughout the exercise, and the knee of your stance leg should stay in line with your foot rather than collapsing inward. If you don't have a plyometric box, you can do this on a staircase step. Work toward two to three sets with ten to fifteen repetitions.

KICKING AND PASSING POWER

Soccer kicks, whether they are passes or shots on goal, require stability in the stance leg and power through the kicking leg. Strength through the torso also provides balance and power. With training, teenage players can reach kicking speeds of 50 to 64 miles per hour (80–103 kmh).[6] Professional players can kick at speeds of more than 70 miles per hour (113 kmh).[7]

There are some exercises that work to train stance-leg stability, kicking-leg power, and torso engagement all at the same time. Lunges and single-leg squats are a common examples. Another example is the standing fire hydrant.

To begin the standing fire hydrant, stand and balance on one leg with your knee slightly bent. Bend your other knee to a 90-degree angle with your foot behind your body. Lean slightly forward while keeping a neutral spine and level hips. Placing your hands on your hips can help gauge whether they are level.

Squeeze your glutes while keeping the 90-degree bend in your lifted leg, and raise it out to the side. Make sure your lifted knee does not move forward or backward

Soccer players plant their nonkicking leg next to the ball before following through.

as you raise it to the side. Engage your core and stance leg to balance and stay centered over your stance leg. Work up to holding the position for one minute. Add an elastic band around your thighs for additional resistance.

Plyometric drills build strength. They also incorporate coordination for balance and soccer-specific movement patterns for kicking. Butt kicks are one example. To perform them, run forward slowly, drawing the heel of your back leg to your glutes while remaining upright.

Skipping kicks are another plyometric drill. When landing on one leg in a skip, pull your other leg into a butt kick. As you hop forward with the same leg on the ground, draw your back leg's knee forward to about hip height then extend the leg into a kick. Draw your

Skipping improves leg strength, balance, and coordination.

kicking leg back so it lands in a safe position to spring into the next skip. Work toward performing these skips for 20 yards (18.2 m) and two to three sets.

QUICKNESS AND AGILITY IN DRIBBLING

Even elite soccer players regularly practice basic dribbling. Professional soccer player Megan Montefusco says, "When I step out on the field, I know that if I'm building positive habits and I'm doing the same thing over and over and over, it's going to pay off."[8] Drills for quick and agile footwork support dribbling. Drills with balls provide benefits that transfer directly to soccer.

Toe touches are one of the easiest ball drills for quick, agile footwork. Leave the ball stationary in front of you and hop to tap one foot at a time to the top of the ball.

Swing your bent arms at your sides, and stay light on the balls of your feet with your knees slightly bent. To make the drill harder, move in a circle while tapping the top of the ball. Alternate directions for even training. Pushing the ball forward with each foot tap is another progression. Do this for a set number of steps, then reverse direction and pull the ball backward with each toe tap.

A common agility training technique involves using cones to practice changing directions while dribbling. If cones aren't available, trace imaginary figure eights or letters of the alphabet with the ball. An additional drill involves dribbling, passing against a wall, and then controlling the return. This drill integrates reaction training alongside footwork.

Agility ladder exercises are a common complement to dribbling drills because they also build quick and agile footwork. Some of the steps athletes can

UNUSUAL TRAINING

In an article for the website Youth Soccer, professional player Jessica Davis wrote about some of the unusual methods she used when training in her Virginia hometown as a kid. She would use bottles instead of cones for agility drills. She would throw balls uphill to work on gaining height on throw-ins. Other players also had creative methods. The famous soccer star Pelé improvised balls from socks filled with rags or paper when he was growing up in Brazil. Athletes do not always need official equipment to train. They can use creativity and whatever resources they have.

perform through ladders are forward high-knee runs, side-to-side steps, and lateral shuffles. You can practice the same moves without an agility ladder, just make sure to focus on quick movements in a short amount of space.

GOALIE TRAINING

Goalies need foundations in strength, power, and fast footwork like other players do. However, the goalie position is unique in soccer, and goalies spend large portions of training time practicing separately from the rest of the team. Goalkeeping requires skills in agility, quickness, and reading angles. Many goalkeeping drills involve taking angled shots from partners, but there are also drills goalies can do on their own.

Goalkeepers can practice wall drills as a way to improve reflexes, handling skills, and footwork. Toss the ball against the wall at various heights, speeds, and angles. Move your position in relation to the wall to simulate different types of shots. Work up to making 100 catches without stopping and without any drops.

You can also adjust the same drill to use a tennis ball. Using the smaller ball will create a bigger challenge. Stand about four feet (1.2 m) from the wall. Hold the tennis ball in your right hand. Toss the ball against the wall high and to your right so you have to shuffle to catch it overhand. Alternate between tossing left and right.

A goalkeeper must defend 192 square feet (18 sq m) of space to keep balls out of the net.

Hand stretches are important for goalkeepers, since stopping shots can place a lot of strain on their wrists.

Goalies can also create their own circuits for strength and power training. One drill is made of multiple segments that players can put together when they are ready for a challenge. Create a diamond with cones at three of the points and a soccer ball at the fourth. Put the cones several feet apart. You will need enough room between them to perform the actions described in the drill.

PRACTICING ANGLES

Using rope gives a visual for reading angles. Tie one end of a long rope to each goalpost. Grab the middle of the rope and pull it out to create a triangle shape. Move the middle of the rope to various positions around the goal. At each position, put the middle of the rope on the ground with a soccer ball. The triangle now shows the possible shooting angles from each of these positions. The shooting angle is the space on either side of the goalie where a shot could pass through and still land in the goal. Using the rope to visualize these shots can help train goalies to position themselves to narrow these angles.

Start at the first cone and do ten push-ups. In the second segment, stand up and circle around that cone, moving forward, backward, and laterally. Keep your chest squared forward and practice quick footwork. In the third segment, dive toward the second cone as if you're saving a shot on goal. Pop back up, then move to the third cone and dive over it. Next, get back up and dive to cover the ball. Finally, toss the ball in the air and catch it again before it hits the ground.

ARCIA

CHAPTER SIX

BASEBALL AND SOFTBALL TRAINING

Sports professionals frequently use the term *ballistic* to describe baseball and softball movements. Players encounter many gameplay situations that last for a few seconds or less. In those short times, they must be explosive and reactive.

A batter in a Major League Baseball (MLB) game facing a 95-mile-per-hour (153 kmh) fastball has less than 0.4 seconds to decide whether to swing.[1] Fielders face line drives that can travel approximately 100 yards (91 m) in four seconds.[2] Power hitters at professional, college, and high school levels can hit a ball that's going 100 miles per hour (161 kmh) or faster.[3]

Many consider hitting a baseball to be the hardest action to execute in sports.

Baseball and softball players prepare with plyometric drills that require explosive movement and sprinting drills for speed. Training also focuses on building strength and stability to protect the body, especially the throwing arm, through explosive movements. This kind of training benefits all positions, even though baseball and softball feature highly specialized player positions that must also be addressed with individual training. Baseball's essential skills are throwing, pitching, catching, batting, sprinting, jumping, and the ability to change direction.

PITCH COMMUNICATION

Baseball traditionally has used hand signals between coaches, catchers, and pitchers to plan what kind of pitch to throw. In 2022, MLB began allowing teams to use a new technology system, called PitchCom. The system has wristband transmitters and earpiece receivers. In 2023, MLB rules allowed for the pitcher, catcher, and three fielders to have transmitters. Catchers press buttons on the transmitters, which allowed those players wearing receivers to know what pitch was being called. This system is designed to fight sign stealing, which is when opponents track hand signals to gain an advantage. All-Star pitcher Max Scherzer acknowledged the benefits but said, "I also feel like it takes away part of the game."[5]

ARM TRAINING

Personal trainer Paul Rogers writes, "In baseball, your arm is everything, no matter what position you play."[4] Throwing, pitching, and hitting require rapid arm acceleration and deceleration, shoulder

Shoulder and elbow injuries are common for pitchers, especially those who throw exceptionally hard.

rotation, and bending and straightening of the elbow. These motions produce the high-velocity balls that make baseball and softball such exciting sports. At the same time, baseball and softball see more elbow and shoulder injuries than many other sports. Training focuses on strength, range of motion, and stability, especially in the shoulder's rotator cuff, to keep players' arms healthy.

The shoulder is a very mobile ball-and-socket joint. This mobility allows the shoulder a wide range of motion for sport performance, but it also puts the shoulder at risk of injury. The rotator cuff is responsible for moving the arm around the shoulder joint. The rotator cuff consists of four muscles and the tendons that connect those muscles to bone. It holds the ball of the shoulder joint stable in the socket. The rounded top end of the humerus bone of the upper arm is the ball part of the joint, and the shoulder blade is the socket. Training the rotator cuff helps to protect both the shoulder and the elbow.

Players frequently train with elastic bands or tubing to build stability. Cable machines can also be used, but should be set to light weight to avoid overexertion and injury. Exercises include external and internal rotations, extensions, and abduction. For all of these exercises, it is important to maintain good form with your shoulders level and not shrugging upward.

External rotations move the arm out, while internal rotations move it in. For external rotation, anchor an

Bands help baseball and softball pitchers loosen up their arms before they start games.

elastic band across the front of your body at hip height. Grasp the end of the band in one hand. Hold your arm against the side of your body and bend your elbow 90 degrees and your palm facing your body. Keep your arm level as you rotate your forearm out and away from your body; your elbow should stay at 90 degrees throughout the motion. It is important to also place your opposite hand under your armpit for stability.

To perform an internal rotation, set the band up at hip height in front of you. Grasp the band at your side and rotate inward across your body. Place your opposite hand outside the elbow of the moving arm for stability.

Lat extensions, or straight-arm pull-downs, move your arm back. Anchor the middle of the band at shoulder height. Grasp one end in each hand. Begin with your arms straight and raised in front of your body and parallel to the ground. Your palms should face the floor. Squeeze your shoulder blades together as you pull your arms down and back to the sides of your body. Make sure to keep your arms straight.

Abductions move your arm up and away from your body. Anchor the band under your foot and hold the end in the same side's hand. Your arm should be straight and down by your hip. Keep your wrist straight, and bend your elbow slightly so it isn't locked. Raise your arm to the side so it is shoulder height and parallel to the ground.

Pitchers use their legs to drive forward and generate extra power.

Athletes can do these exercises three to four times a week, aiming for three sets of ten to fifteen. The exercises are recommended for both arms, not just your dominant arm. Experienced athletes can incorporate additional exercises, such as overhead triceps extensions and upright rows.

POWER TRAINING WITH PLYOMETRICS

Hitting, pitching, and throwing skills require much more than a person's arms. Power to produce these skills also comes from driving through the legs and rotating through the hips and torso. Base training in leg and core strength provides a foundation for power. Plyometric drills with slam balls and medicine balls are common baseball and softball training methods to convert foundational strength to explosive, full-body movement.

These exercises also train hip-shoulder separation. That is the distance between the hip and shoulder in rotational movements such as batting, pitching, and throwing. Hip-shoulder separation allows space to build speed through the torso and transfer that speed as energy through the arm.

CHANGING VIEWS ON BASEBALL STRENGTH

Nolan Ryan played in the MLB for 27 years. During those years, the hard-throwing pitcher set the league's all-time no-hitter and strikeout records. Ryan attributed his success to strength training. Ryan was drafted in 1965 but did not begin strength training until the 1972 season. Even then, he trained in secret. At the time, baseball professionals believed increased muscle bulk would negatively impact performance. However, Ryan found that strength training prevented fatigue during games and helped him recover more quicky. A conditioning expert hired by the Houston Astros in 1976 credited Ryan with transforming other players' views on strength training.

Shovel passes with a slam ball can be done to target horizontal rotation. Stand near a wall but at least a step away so that there is room to throw. Face sideways, not toward the wall. Hold the ball with both hands by the hip of your leg farther from the wall.

Shovel the ball horizontally across your body and throw it against the wall. Rotation through the hips directs the movement, and weight transfers from one hip to the hip closest to the wall. For proper form, your hips and chest should face the wall when the ball releases. Catch the ball, rotate back to the starting position, and repeat the pass. Keep your back straight and your core braced throughout to prevent overrotating. Perform the move on both sides for balanced training.

QUICKNESS FROM THE ANKLES

Many sports, including baseball and softball, use pogo jumps as a foundation for quickness. Pogo jumps are fast, upward pops with movement coming from the foot and ankle. They train athletes to minimize ground contact time. Minimizing contact time is key to quick and agile movements. For basic pogo jumps, stand in place and bounce through the balls of your feet. Avoid bending your knees and hips. Aim for sets of ten to 20. There are single-leg and lateral variations. In lateral variations, athletes move left or right during the jumps.

Single-leg rotational side slams focus on vertical and diagonal movement. Start by balancing on whichever leg drives forward when hitting or throwing. If you are right-handed, this would be your left leg. Keep your other leg bent behind your body with your foot off the ground. Hold a slam ball in both hands near the hip of your standing leg. Rotate to sweep the ball over your opposite shoulder, then slam the ball down and diagonally so it lands in front of your standing leg.

Medicine ball throws and slams can enhance power in both the arms and legs.

FITNESS SNAPSHOT

LATERAL SHUFFLE

Engage core

Face forward

Keep weight centered, even when changing direction

Hinge at hips in a half squat

Stay light on toes

Keep feet wide

Your hips and chest should direct the movement in this drill too.

Recommended sets and repetitions for medicine and slam ball throws depend on where you are in your training cycle. In early training to prepare for the season, experts suggest doing two different kinds of throws two to three times per week. They recommend two to three sets of five to six repetitions. Experts suggest using a ball weighing between four and eight pounds (1.8 and 3.6 kg), but it could be lighter depending on your size and experience.[6]

AGILITY AND QUICKNESS

Players at all positions can develop a foundation for speed with sprinting drills. These drills should focus on proper running mechanics and safe, fast acceleration and deceleration. Basic linear sprint drills can use progressions of 30, 90, and 180 feet (9, 27, and 55 m). In MLB, bases are 90 feet (27 m) apart.[7] Basepaths for players older than age 13 can be 70 to 90 feet (21–27 m).[8] Setting up cones or poles to weave through integrates more agility into sprinting work, and sprinting along the curve from first base to third base trains players to take curves while moving at high speed.

For the fast side-to-side movements baseball demands, players train their lateral acceleration and deceleration. Short lateral shuffles provide a basis for this training. Begin at a center cone, shuffle to one side, and then shuffle across to the other side. Face forward the whole time and keep your feet wide without any crossover. To incorporate crossover footwork, lateral shuffle in one direction and perform crossover steps to return in the opposite direction. You can also change the distance between cones or the speed of the drill to increase the difficulty.

You can mix lateral shuffles with forward sprints to mimic turns required in games. For this drill, lateral shuffle for five yards (4.6 m) then turn 90 degrees and sprint five yards (4.6 m) in the same direction. For example, if you shuffle to the right of a cone, you would also sprint that way. Push off your left leg to make the turn and square your shoulders forward.

For a variation that includes a full change of direction, shuffle laterally for five yards (4.6 m) in one direction. Then turn 180 degrees to face the opposite way. After that, sprint ten yards (9 m) straight ahead.

You can incorporate movements in which your hands touch the ground to add a greater agility challenge to these drills. That will help you prepare for gameplay movements such as fielding a ground ball and turning to throw or turning back and diving to a base. You can begin one drill by facing forward and kneeling on one knee. Push through your legs to stand and simultaneously turn

Infielders need quick reactions to reach hard-hit balls to either side of their position.

to sprint. Sprint 2.5 yards (2.3 m), lunge to touch a cone with one hand, and then turn quickly to sprint five yards (4.6 m) in the opposite direction. Be sure to practice equally on each leg.

These agility and quickness drills build skills all players need, but training should also focus on position-specific demands. Infielders may spend more time training with a focus on lateral acceleration and deceleration. Outfielders may spend more time on linear acceleration training. Catchers may spend more time on drills that begin with quick bursts from squat stance. However, there are many general drills that can help provide a baseline for successful baseball and softball training.

97
CCM
C
97
CCM
CCM
CCM
JETSPEED

ICE HOCKEY TRAINING

Modern ice hockey emerged in the 1870s in Montreal, Canada. It drew from a long history of earlier versions of the game. Field hockey was played on dry land. It was later adapted onto the ice into a game known as shinny. Shinny looked much like hockey does today, but games were played on large open ice surfaces and without formal positions. Ice hockey also drew from rugby and lacrosse.

Today, ice hockey is considered one of the major team sports in North America. Essential skills in hockey include skating, puck control, passing and receiving, shooting, defending, and goaltending. In an academic article about measuring hockey performance, sports medicine researchers describe skating in ice hockey as

National Hockey League (NHL) superstar Connor McDavid was once clocked skating 25 miles per hour (40 kmh) in a game.

HIP MOBILITY AND FLEXIBILITY

Hockey players push into their hips for speed and power in their skating. Training incorporates mobility and flexibility exercises to reduce injury risk from tightness in the hips. This kind of training also promotes agility and quickness. Common dynamic exercises to open and warm up the hips are leg swings and hip abduction walks.

"a combination of speed, strength, power, and balance."[1]

SKATING STRENGTH AND AGILITY

Off-ice training helps build the strength required for powerful skating performance. As in other sports, hockey training conditions the upper body, lower body, back, and core. There is also special emphasis on single-leg exercises for strength and balance.

Single-leg strength training prepares the body for various gameplay movements, including linear strides, curves, and sharp turns. Personal trainer Brian Sutton explains that "loading of the legs is seldom equal" throughout these movements.[2] As a result, each leg needs the ability to support large workloads.

Walking lunges and split squats are a few of the exercises that provide a foundation for single-leg strength and balance. Lunges and squats also have variations that can target hip strength alongside single-leg work. For example, curtsy squats resemble hockey's crossover stride, and they engage the hip adductors located near the inner thighs.

Walking lunges primarily strengthen the calves, glutes, hamstrings, and quadriceps.

FITNESS SNAPSHOT

ROMANIAN DEAD LIFT

Bend as low as possible while keeping back straight

Keep shoulders back

Hinge at hips

Engage core muscles

Use weights if desired

Knees can be slightly bent

Keep body weight back in the heels

To perform curtsy squats, squat on one leg while passing your other leg behind your body. This should create the curtsying motion that gives the exercise its name. Your hips should remain level and facing forward throughout the motion. The knee of your stance leg should stay in line with your foot without collapsing inward. Aim for two sets of ten on each side.

TRAINING EQUIPMENT WITH DYNAMIC SURFACES

Several types of training equipment provide an unstable surface for stability work. Balance boards, BOSU balls, balance pads, and fitters are examples. The unstable surface is called a dynamic surface, and it increases proprioception, which is an athlete's awareness of body position. This surface also builds strength, stability, and mobility in the ankle's muscles, ligaments, and tendons. Athletes can perform shallow squats, lunges, Pallof presses, and other exercises with various kinds of balance equipment. Slide boards are another tool. They have a smooth surface with low friction, similar to ice. Athletes can plant one leg on the ground and slide the other along the board like lateral lunges and back lunges.

Romanian dead lift (RDL) variations are also common exercises for single-leg strength and balance. They are named in honor of Romanian weight lifter Nicu Vlad, who developed the exercise with his coach. RDLs use a hip-hinging movement and target the hamstrings and glutes.

Double-leg RDLs are great for focusing on the basics of the exercise. Using two legs will still involve some balance work. Start by standing straight up with your feet shoulder-width apart. Lower your upper body by bending at the hips while keeping your back and legs straight. When you feel your hamstrings begin to stretch, rise back up to your original standing position by squeezing your glutes together and pushing your hips forward. Aim to do six to ten repetitions.

To make the exercise more difficult, place a kettlebell or weight between your feet. Bend down to pick up the weight, and hold it with your arms hanging down in front of you as you rise back up. There are also single-leg variations of RDLs. These can be done with or without weights.

Finally, hockey players can employ various plyometric drills. The single-leg hurdle hop is a common exercise. Place a small box or hurdle on the ground at a height you can comfortably jump over. Stand next to the hurdle, facing sideways and not toward the hurdle. Keep one leg bent and slightly raised

BODY CHECKING

USA Hockey rules prohibit body checking for athletes ages 12 and younger, and most women's hockey organizations do not allow body checking at all. Some argue that the rule differences for men and women are unfair. In 2022, the Swedish Women's Hockey League decided to permit body checking in games. A year later, the Professional Women's Hockey League in the United States and Canada began play. It allowed for body checking if a player was trying to gain possession of the puck. Others argue that games are competitive and physical enough without expanding body checking rules.

Working with cones or other obstacles helps players practice stickhandling in crowded spaces.

behind your body and hop laterally over the hurdle. In one variation, your inside leg is raised off the ground. In another variation, your outside leg is raised off the ground. These variations challenge different parts of the legs and hips. You can also do quick alternating crossover hop steps over the hurdle. If no hurdle is available, perform the drills without it but aim for the height that you would if the hurdle were there.

STICKHANDLING, PASSING, AND SHOOTING

Hockey training professionals emphasize stickhandling is the foundation for all skills in puck control, passing,

Former NHL defenseman Zdeno Chára had one of the hardest slap shots of all time. His record was 108.8 miles per hour (175.1 kmh).

and shooting. Drills that promote quick hands improve stickhandling, and agility drills involving the whole body build from there. Athletes can practice both types of drills on and off the ice.

The quick hands drill emphasizes smooth, rolling wrist rotation with minimal arm movement. For basic practice, take an athletic stance with gloves on, a stick in your hands, and a puck or ball in front of you. Remain stationary while moving the stick over the puck or ball. Tap your stick to the ground with light, rapid touches.

Practice quick wrist rotation with the stick directly in front of your body then off to each side. Focusing on repetition and form is key. From there, you can create obstacle courses with cones or pucks to incorporate footwork, agility, and other skills.

Stickhandling trains puck control, and strength provides the power for passing and hard shots. The fastest slap shots in professional hockey travel more than 100 miles per hour (161 kmh).[3] In addition to strength, rotation through the trunk and shoulders also helps generate this kind of speed and power.

Additional upper body exercises support passing ability and shooting power. Common exercises are dumbbell bench presses and incline bench presses, rows, lat pulldowns, push-ups, and pull-ups. Experienced athletes can incorporate exercises that challenge skills of balance, upper body strength, core strength, and single-leg strength all at once. RDLs with a row are an example.

GOALIE TRAINING

Hockey goalies benefit from much of the same training as other players. However, like goalies in other sports, they also face unique demands and spend portions of training time practicing on their own. Goalies work on mental drills that enhance body positioning, hand-eye coordination, and mental concentration. Physical drills can build up a goalie's leg strength and stamina as well as overall agility, flexibility, and quickness.

Quick, agile recovery ability allows goalies to get back into a ready stance after dropping down to make a save. This ability is essential because goalies need to rapidly recover, react, and transition instantly into a new movement. One common drill is moving from a half-kneeling position into a lateral jump.

Start by kneeling on your left knee with your right leg bent in front of you. Push off your right foot as you lift your left leg off the ground. Maintaining a half-squat, hop sideways and land on your left foot. Return to the starting position and repeat that same motion. Complete your desired number of reps on one side before switching directions.

Goaltenders need strong legs to push off from side to side as they react to shots.

Since goalies have to track speeding pucks flying through crowds of players, excellent hand-eye coordination is essential. There are many on-ice drills to hone this ability. There are also off-ice drills that can be done without a partner.

Begin one drill by standing and underhand tossing a tennis ball against a wall. Catch the rebound with one hand. Vary the height, speed, and angle of the catch and alternate the tossing hand. You can also practice throwing the ball with one hand and catching with the other.

By staying square to shots, goalkeepers can make saves with less effort, and they can control rebounds better.

As you progress through the drill, begin dropping down to a knee. For example, when you throw and catch the ball, drop down to your right knee. Then bring your left knee down so you are on both knees. Then rise back up, starting with your left leg, and then your right.

Cone agility drills provide additional angle work for goalies. In the four-cone drill, cones are placed about ten feet (3 m) apart in a box shape. Move quickly from cone to cone, turning your body and squaring to the cone as if it were the puck. Practicing these movements will help you narrow the shooting angles available to offensive players.

MENTAL STRENGTH

Legendary goaltender Jacques Plante once said of the position, "Can you imagine a job where every time you make a mistake, a red light goes on and 15,000 people stand up and cheer?"[4] Hockey goaltenders face a lot of pressure. Professionals spend significant time honing the mental skills to play the position. Many employ techniques such as visualization or meditation to help them prepare for games. These can be used to picture making saves, recover when goals are allowed, or simply clear their minds.

Goaltending coach Austin Christopher recommends simple five- to ten-minute meditation sessions as a key tool to help goaltenders focus. Begin by shutting your eyes and inhaling for three seconds while focusing on your breathing. Keep that focus as you exhale for four seconds. "Count them. This keeps you focused on your breathing, which basically is the only thing happening at that very moment, and it keeps you centered," says Christopher.[5] On the ice, that can translate to improved focus on the puck and the job of stopping shots.

ESSENTIAL FACTS

What Is Sports Training?

- Sports training develops the skills athletes need for a particular sport.
- Periodization involves progressive training over weeks or months to prepare for a competitive season or event.
- Sports training focuses on strength, agility, and quickness through combinations of aerobic training, anaerobic training, and skill drills.
- Athletes train in gyms and at sport-specific fields, courts, rinks, or pools.
- Well-designed sports programs integrate guidance for mental health, nutrition, and rest to complement physical training in all phases and to support athletes.

Benefits of Sports Training

- Improved performance and reduced risk of injury.
- Stronger bones, connective tissue, and muscles.
- Improved blood flow to muscles and more efficient oxygen use.
- More endurance and greater recovery ability.
- Greater explosiveness and more powerful movements.

Quote

"When I step out on the field, I know that if I'm building positive habits and I'm doing the same thing over and over and over, it's going to pay off."

—Megan Montefusco, professional soccer player

GLOSSARY

abduction

The movement of a limb away from another part of the body, usually the body's midline.

agility

The ability to move dynamically with balance and control and react quickly.

cardiovascular

Relating to the heart and blood vessels.

cross-training

Exercise training in an activity other than the athlete's primary sport.

dietician

A health professional with expertise in nutrition.

hormone

A chemical produced by the body that creates various effects throughout the body.

lateral

Sideways.

macronutrient

A nutrient needed in large amounts, including carbohydrates, fats, and protein.

medicine ball

A heavy ball used for workouts.

metabolize

To process for the use of turning one material into another.

optimal

As good as possible.

plyometric

Relating to exercises involving quick stretching and contracting of muscles, such as jumps.

skeletal muscle

A muscle attached to bone.

tendon

A cord of tissue that connects muscle to bone.

volume

Amount or quantity.

ADDITIONAL RESOURCES

Selected Bibliography

Chapman, Stacey, Edward Derse, and Jacqueline Hanson, editors. *Soccer Coaching Manual*. LA84 Foundation, 2012, la84.org.

Coleman, A. Eugene, and David J. Szymanski, editors. *Strength Training for Baseball*. Human Kinetics, 2022.

Roque, Elaine, and Jacqueline Hansen, editors. *Volleyball Coaching Manual*. LA84 Foundation, 2012, la84.org.

"Training at Home: Age-Specific Training." *USA Hockey*, n.d., usahockey.com. Accessed 6 Nov. 2023.

Further Readings

Best, Michael T. *Excelling in Hockey*. ReferencePoint, 2020.

Roggio, Sarah. *Strength Training*. Abdo, 2025.

Roland, James. *The Science and Technology of Soccer*. ReferencePoint, 2020.

Online Resources

To learn more about sports training, please visit **abdobooklinks.com** or scan this QR code. These links are routinely monitored and updated to provide the most current information available.

More Information

For more information on this subject, contact or visit the following organizations:

LA84 Foundation

2141 W. Adams Blvd.
Los Angeles, CA 90018
la84.org/contact/

The LA84 Foundation works to make sports safe and accessible for all youth Para athletes and athletes. It trains coaches, promotes research, holds events, and offers grants.

National Athletic Trainers' Association (NATA)

1620 Valwood Pkwy., Ste. 115
Carrollton, TX 75006
nata.org

The National Athletic Trainers' Association promotes research and education in athletic training. NATA also advocates for both state and federal legislation benefiting trainers and promotes youth sports safety initiatives.

Sports Performance and Research Center

Emory University School of Medicine
James B. Williams Medical Education Building
100 Woodruff Cir.
Atlanta, GA 30322
med.emory.edu/departments/orthopaedics/research/sparc

Emory University's Sports Performance and Research Center (SPARC) researches injury diagnosis and prevention in youth sports.

SOURCE NOTES

Chapter 1. Training on the Basketball Court

1. Frank L. Smoll. "How to Develop Mentally Tough Young Athletes." *Psychology Today*, 5 Oct. 2015, psychologytoday.com. Accessed 27 Feb. 2024.

Chapter 2. What Is Sports Training?

1. Gabrielle Kassel. "How Periodization Training Can Help You Reach Your Goals Faster." *Shape*, 27 Apr. 2022, shape.com. Accessed 2 Feb. 2024.

2. Kit Ramgopal. "Virtual Reality Companies Are Changing How Athletes See Practice." *New York Times*, 24 Nov. 2017, nytimes.com. Accessed 2 Feb. 2024.

Chapter 3. Sports Training and the Body

1. "Bone Density and Weight-Bearing Exercise." *Orthopedic & Sports Medicine Institute*, n.d., osmifw.com. Accessed 26 Feb. 2024.

2. Phil Goulding. "What Is Aerobic vs. Anaerobic Training." *Nuffield Health*, 23 Oct. 2023, nuffieldhealth.com. Accessed 2 Feb. 2024.

3. "How Microtears Help You to Build Muscle Mass." *Science of Health*, 5 Feb. 2018, uhhospitals.org. Accessed 2 Feb. 2024.

4. Laura K. Purcell. "Sport Nutrition for Young Athletes." *Paediatrics and Child Health*, vol. 18, no. 4, April 2013, ncbi.nlm.nih.gov. Accessed 2 Feb. 2024.

5. Heather Mangieri. "Healthy Hydration for Young Athletes." *National Athletic Trainers' Association News*, July 2018, nata.org. Accessed 2 Feb. 2024.

6. Allison Brager. "Athlete Recovery Techniques to Achieve Peak Performance." *National Academy of Sports Medicine*, n.d., nasm.org. Accessed 2 Feb. 2024.

7. David Waldstein. "Grab and Go: How Sticky Gloves Have Changed Football." *New York Times*, 20 Jan. 2019, nytimes.com. Accessed 2 Feb. 2024.

8. Jacob Moreton. "Athletes Using High-Tech Shoes Are 'Cheating', Says Former Marathon World Record Holder." *Runners World*, 4 May 2021, runnersworld.com. Accessed 2 Feb. 2024.

Chapter 4. Volleyball Training

1. Brandon Hall. "Basketball Court Dimensions and Hoop Height: A Quick Guide." *Stack*, 12 Oct. 2010, stack.com. Accessed 2 Feb. 2024.

2. Eli Straw. "Sports Visualization Techniques for Athletes." *Success Starts Within*, 19 Jan. 2024, successstartswithin.com. Accessed 27 Feb. 2024.

3. Brenna Berkimer. "How to Increase Your Vertical for Volleyball." *NBC Camps*, 5 Oct. 2023, nbccamps.com. Accessed 2 Feb. 2024.

4. Marie Zidek. "10 Volleyball-Specific Strength Exercises & Workouts." *Art of Coaching Volleyball*, 20 Dec. 2016, theartofcoachingvolleyball.com. Accessed 2 Feb. 2024.

Chapter 5. Soccer Training

1. "Soccer." *Library of Congress Research Guides*, n.d., guides.loc.gov. Accessed 2 Feb. 2024.

2. "Average Distance Ran in a Soccer Game: Each Position." *Progressive Soccer Training*, n.d., Accessed 2 Feb. 2024.

3. Stacey Chapman, Edward Derse, and Jacqueline Hanson, editors. *Soccer Coaching Manual*. LA84 Foundation, 2012, la84.org

4. Chapman, et al., *Soccer Coaching Manual*.

5. Damian James Harper and John Kiely. "Damaging Nature of Decelerations: Do We Adequately Prepare Players?" *BMJ Open Sport & Exercise Medicine*, vol. 4, no. 1, 6 Aug. 2018, bmjopensem.bmj.com. Accessed 27 Feb. 2024.

6. Ante Rađa, et al. "The Ball Kicking Speed: A New, Efficient Performance Indicator in Youth Soccer." *PLoS One*, vol. 15, no. 5, 17 May 2019, ncbi.nlm.nih.gov. Accessed 2 Feb. 2024.

7. "Ball Kicking Speed."

8. "Soccer Dribbling 101: Run These Drills." *Adidas*, Mar. 2022, adidas.com. Accessed 2 Feb. 2024.

SOURCE NOTES CONTINUED

Chapter 6. Baseball and Softball Training

1. "How a Baseball Batter's Brain Reacts to a Fast Pitch." *NPR*, 3 Sept. 2016, npr.org. Accessed 2 Feb. 2024.

2. "The Physics of Baseball." *Steve O's Umpire Resources*, n.d., stevetheump.com. Accessed 2 Feb. 2024.

3. Kristen Conti. "Here Are the Hardest-Hit Balls in MLB History." *NBC Sports Chicago*, 24 Aug. 2022, nbcsportschicago.com. Accessed 2 Feb. 2024.

4. Justin Tasch. "Mets' Max Scherzer After Using PitchCom for First Time: 'Should Be Illegal'." *New York Post*, 28 Jul. 2022, nypost.com. Accessed 2 Feb. 2024.

5. Paul Rogers. "A General Weight Training Program for Baseball." *Verywell Fit*, 16 Sept. 2022, verywellfit.com. Accessed 2 Feb. 2024.

6. "Top 6 Med Ball Drills for Pitchers and Players." *Rockland Peak Performance*, 23 Jul. 2021, rocklandpeakperformance.com. Accessed 27 Feb. 2024.

7. "Field Dimensions." *Major League Baseball*, n.d., mlb.com. Accessed 2 Feb. 2024.

8. "Field Specifications." *Little League*, n.d., littleleague.org. Accessed 2 Feb. 2024.

Chapter 7. Ice Hockey Training

1. David A. Krause, et al. "Relationship of Off-Ice and On-Ice Performance Measures in High School Male Hockey Players." *Journal of Strength and Conditioning Research*, vol. 26, no. 5, May 2012, journals.lww.com. Accessed 2 Feb. 2024.

2. Paul Rogers. "A General Ice Hockey Weight Training Program." *Verywell Fit*, 22 Feb. 2020, verywellfit.com. Accessed 2 Feb. 2024.

3. Scott Weldon. "NHL: 25 Hardest Slap Shots in the History of Hockey." *Bleacher Report*, 21 May 2011, bleacherreport.com. Accessed 2 Feb. 2024.

4. Brion O'Connor. "BU Netminder Proves Mentality Is Key for Hockey Goalies at All Levels." *Sports Illustrated,* 28 Apr. 2015, si.com. Accessed 2 Feb. 2024.

5. "Meditation and Breathing." *YouTube*, uploaded by The Mental Goalie School, 18 Sept. 2019, youtube.com. Accessed 2 Feb. 2024.

INDEX

acceleration, 61–63, 74
- lateral acceleration, 83, 85

adaptations, 31, 33, 36–37
aerobic, 21–23, 31–35, 37, 58
agility, 20, 24–26, 49, 52, 61, 67–68, 83–85, 88, 95–96, 98
anaerobic, 31, 34–36, 37

balance, 11, 20, 24, 49–50, 51, 64–66, 88, 91, 96
baseball, 27, 28, 43, 73–75, 79, 80, 83, 85
basketball, 6, 9–10, 13, 29, 38, 42, 45–46
bench presses, 95
biomechanics, 27, 38
biometrics, 27
body weight, 5, 26, 52, 90
box jumps, 24
boxing, 18
burpees, 5
butt kicks, 65

calf raises, 23
calves, 8, 50
carbohydrates, 37–38
cardio, 25
chest presses, 23
compound exercises, 22–23
coordination, 20, 65
core, 11, 49–50, 52–55, 65, 78, 80, 82, 88, 90, 96
cross-training, 25
cuju, 18
cycling, 23

dance, 25
deceleration, 61–63, 73, 84
- lateral deceleration, 83, 85

double-leg hops, 24, 52
dumbbells, 52, 54, 58, 95

endurance, 19, 21, 23, 32, 34
Euro hop step, 9

Fartlek runs, 61
fast-twitch muscle fibers, 33–34, 36
fatigue, 25, 27, 79
flexibility, 20, 25, 50, 88, 96
football, 22, 25, 27, 28–29, 42
footwork, 14, 19, 25, 47–49, 66–68, 71, 84, 95

glucose, 32, 34
glutes, 50, 64–65, 91–92
glycolysis, 34–35
gyms, 26–27

hamstrings, 8, 23, 50, 91–92
hand-eye coordination, 96–97
haptic technology, 29
heart rate, 27, 35
high intensity, 23, 34–36, 37, 61
hips, 8, 48, 52–53, 54, 62–64, 78–80, 82, 83, 88, 90, 91–93
hip-shoulder separation, 79
hormones, 40
hydration, 37–40
hypertrophy, 36

ice hockey, 87–88, 92–93, 96, 99
injuries, 20, 21, 25, 29, 31, 36–37, 38, 58, 62, 75–76, 88
isolation exercises, 22–23

kettlebells, 26, 92

lacrosse, 27, 87
lat pulldowns, 95
lateral shuffles, 7–8, 68, 83–84

ligaments, 10, 22, 38, 61, 91
low impact, 45
low intensity, 37
lunges, 5, 23, 49–50, 52, 64, 88, 91

medicine balls, 10, 26, 52, 54, 79, 83
meditation, 99
microtears, 36
mobility, 20, 25, 41, 50, 75, 88, 91
muscle memory, 38

neck muscles, 58
nutrition, 20, 25, 37–39

obliques, 50
overhead triceps extensions, 78

Pallof presses, 91
Pasuckquakkohowog, 57
periodization, 20–21, 25
Pilates, 25
planks, 5, 23
plyometrics, 20, 23–24, 26, 34, 61, 63–65, 74, 79, 92
power, 9, 11, 14–15, 22, 24–25, 34, 45, 47, 50, 52–53, 61, 63–64, 68, 71, 73, 78–79, 88, 95
prehabilitation, 20
pull-ups, 95
push-ups, 5, 10, 23, 26, 71, 95

quadriceps, 8, 23, 50, 63
quickness, 15, 24–26, 47, 58, 68, 80, 85, 88, 96

range of motion, 75
reactions, 15, 29, 41, 43, 47–48, 67
recovery, 20–22, 25, 31, 33–34, 36–38, 40–41, 79
reflexes, 57, 68
rest, 7, 9–10, 20, 25, 59
Romanian dead lifts (RDLs), 91–92, 96
rotator cuff, 75–76
rows, 23, 95
  upright rows, 78
rugby, 25, 87
running, 16, 18–19, 22–23, 27, 34, 42, 47, 57–58, 61, 83
  jogging, 6, 37, 61
  shuttle runs, 9
  sprinting, 7, 25–26, 37, 58–59, 61, 74, 83–85

shoulder shrugs, 58
skiing, 25
slam balls, 54, 79–80, 83
sleep, 37, 40–41
slow-twitch muscle fibers, 33–34
soccer, 18, 25, 29, 57, 58, 61, 64–66, 67, 68, 71
softball, 27, 73–75, 79, 80, 85
speed, 19, 22, 24, 37, 58–59, 61, 74, 83, 88, 95
squats, 5, 23, 49–50, 63–64, 88, 91
stability, 20, 33, 52, 63–64, 74–77, 91
stamina, 18, 58, 96
strength training, 19–20, 22–23, 79, 88
stretching, 6, 37, 41
swimming, 19, 23, 25, 27

T drill, 6, 10
tendons, 10, 22, 34, 61, 75, 91

virtual reality (VR), 28–29
visualization, 28, 47, 71, 99
volleyball, 38, 45–46, 48–50, 52
Volleyball Skills & Drills, 46

yoga, 25, 41

ABOUT THE AUTHOR

Rebecca Morris

Rebecca Morris is the author of several nonfiction books for students. She has degrees in English, international relations, and comparative humanities. She played volleyball in high school and enjoys 5K and 10K running.